How To Build A Superhero

Jason E Oliver

Sula Too Publishing

How To Build A Superhero

Jason E Oliver

Copyright © 2020 Jason E Oliver.

All rights reserved. No part of this publication may be reproduced, stored in a retrieval system or transmitted in any form or by any means, electronic, mechanical, photocopying, recording or otherwise without the prior permission of the publisher.

ISBN-978-1-7358398-0-6 Paperback
ISBN-978-1-7358398-1-3 eBook
Library of Congress Control Number: 2020946559

Self help, motivation

Published by Sula Too Publishing
Tampa Florida

For general information,
please contact Sula Too Publishing

www.sulatoo.com/publishing

Backcover note: The principles outlined in this book is what Johnnie applied to start her journey to becoming a registered nurse. In October 2020, shortly before the release of this book, Johnnie passed her exams and is now a certified registered nurse. She is not regretting a single step.

Author's Message and Dedication

I am greatly excited that this book is now a part of your library. What I have given you in this writing comes from my own personal experience of developing the superhero in me. I am still on the journey to becoming legendary however I feel at this point, I am able to start to share and inspire you with some of the knowledge and wisdom that I have gained. It is my hope that this book serves you and allows you to realize and unleash the superhero within. In turn, your heroism serves and saves others.

I dedicate this book to my circle:

My God, My Lord, My Redeemer, My Comforter who has never failed me and never forsake me. You have continued to give me more knowledge, wisdom, and insight as I have sought after you. May I follow as you lead, have my back as I lead, and walk beside me when I need guidance.

My wife, Jennifer, who has encouraged me through all of the stages of my growth as a friend and husband. Times when I have fallen to my knees, she's taken on the fight and allowed me to catch my breath and bearings so that I can get up and fight harder and stronger. She did not let me stay down for long.

My boys, Jason & Joel, who from the first announcement of their coming forced me to want to change my life for the better. I have a greater reason than my own to live and serve to my fullest potential.

My encompassing circle of friends and family. ADAAM Kings and Sister Queens who continually inspire, enforce accountability, and enlighten me to what the world needs and encourage me to continue aiming for the stars and to hit nothing less than the moon.

To you, the reader. The world is desperate for more real-life heroes. I am in utter excitement to see you to become your best superhero self. Don't play small with your heroism.

With love,
Jason

Contents

Chapter I   The Conflict   08

Chapter II   The Clarity   13

Chapter III   The Character   19

Chapter IV   The Belt   23

Chapter V   The Symbol   28

Chapter VI   The Shoes   34

Chapter VII   The Shield   39

Chapter VIII The Helmet   45

Chapter IX   The Weapon   50

Chapter X   The Communication   56

Chapter XI   Becoming The Superhero of You   61

CHAPTER I

The Conflict

The world is huge and too many people need saving for you to be playing small with your heroism." Jason E Oliver

Either you are with us or you are against us. This phrase normally alludes to the fact that a conflict is afoot. In today's world, conflict is so prevalent that it is strange to hear good news. For thousands of years we have read, heard, and seen countries in civil unrest and religious wars. Unfortunately, there is the long-standing strife between races. I wonder how that could be when in truth we're considered one under the human race in more conversations than not. And now we are seeing this old conflict played out in our homes, schools, places of employment and at our local, state, and federal government. This conflict is a fight between truth, personal opinion, perception, false narratives, generational lies, and blatant misinformation.

Since the beginning of time humans have always struggled and fought with those who are different. Conflict starts when two or more sides have a serious disagreement on an issue and cannot, or are unwilling to, come to a mutual resolution. The gap between dispute and resolution forces each side to come face to face with their current position and where they want to be in the future. To resolve conflict, there must be a change or compromise on both sides to garner peace. We live in a world where some type of forceful action is used to resolve but this does not necessarily bring peace to the situation.

The difficulty of conflict resolution is change. In most cases it's perceived that one side is right while the other is wrong. In other cases, one side is trying to push their agenda while promoting the benefits of that said narrative. True change means positive growth. In order for that growth to take place, the need to be right and validated needs to be laid aside. There must be a shift from the comfort zone to adapt a new, challenging method or path. And let's face it, none of us like to be uncomfortable for any reason. So instead of making the necessary changes or compromises, we would prefer someone or something else initiate the change, resolve the conflict, and make the matter more comfortable without us having to lift a finger. This is why the pharmaceutical industry is so successful. We as humans would rather purchase pills with the expectation of losing 50 pounds in seven days rather than change our eating habits, drink more water, and exercise more frequently. To become our best selves, the superhero of our own story, we need to look at change in a more positive light. It has to be looked at as the way to bring about what it is that we truly want.

In the last 100+ years, conflict has been more prominent in our lives with a decent amount of people alive now who were babies when the first World War began. We have read about different wars in history books however now with generations of people living longer, we are not far removed from knowing people, real life superheroes, and hearing stories of their experiences in those wars. With technology advancement in warfare and countries racing to be a superpower, it is at this point when man's fascination with superheroes begins. For generations, fictitious superheroes in comic books have satisfied man's need for comfort in very dark situations. And to see recent box office superhero hits that have been created, it is no surprise that we continue to seek ways to resolve conflicts like they do. How will Superman or The Justice League band together to win the fight against a seemingly unstoppable evil and bring comfort and peace to the world. It's my belief that the number one reason people are attracted to superheroes is because of the hope, courage, and strength they represent. There is also the level of safety that seems to abound in their presence.

In the newer Superman movies, we learn that the "S" on his chest is not a letter but a symbol of hope. When the Bat signal shines brightly in the night sky, it signifies hope for Gotham and justice to be served. People love their superheroes because they are not pushing an agenda of control but rather, they are pushing truth, hope, and encouragement that the citizens desire & deserve.

So many people are losing hope in the world today. It is hard to believe we each are extraordinary, so we look for it in others like sports figures, celebrities, and political leaders. Over the years people have looked to superheroes to replace their own inhibitions and make fears go away. People look to these superhuman "beings" because they possess the positive attributes that they too would like to have, but they do not want the responsibility, accountability and are too fearful to move from their comfort zones. We have become so dependent on the superhuman being that we have forgotten that we possess the attributes that we admire in our superheroes. Qualities like will power, determination, leadership, responsibility, self-motivation, and focus, just to name a few. These same attributes are in the most successful people we see and read about on a daily basis. Our thoughts about them is that they are special and were born that way. However, we fail to realize that almost every single superhero and almost every single successful person was not born with a silver spoon. They were regular people who were made uncomfortable and got out of their comfort zone willingly or sometimes unwillingly at some point in their lives. And it was that state that eventually brought forth change in the character that we today do so admire.

Then this question remains, are superheroes born or created? I believe it is both and neither. I say neither because the answer I prefer to use is that they're developed. Most superheroes encountered a catalyst that jump-started their personal development towards superhero status. If Superman's planet had never been destroyed, he might have lived a normal life, just an average Joe never realizing his great powers, gifts, and potential for earth. If Bruce Wayne never lost his parents, he might have grown up a snobby, rich kid who took over the family business anyway and have been a total miscreant not liked by anyone. Superman and

Batman are both examples of superheroes born and created. The one thing they shared is that they both had to be developed. The start of that development is normally birthed through some adversity. There is a quote by Bill Wilson that says, "To the world you may be one person, but to one person you are the world." When a superhero is being developed, that quote is amplified and may read "to the world you may be one person, and to many people you are the world." The adversity you go through in life is meant for you to grow through and overcome so that you may be a superhero to others.

CHAPTER II

The Clarity

We all have experienced an "ah-ha" moment in our life. It is the moment when something finally makes sense and it all comes together and gives way to clarity. I love Oprah's definition, and I am paraphrasing, "it's a remembering of what you already knew that's articulated in a way that resonates with your own truth". When you have had an "ah ha" moment, there's a rush of freedom, release from worry, building of confidence, increased sense of awareness of self and a cry of happiness to say the least. You start to realize that everything preceding was meant to be and a burst of energy goes into that which you are working on.

In Captain America: The First Avenger, Steven Rogers has "ah ha" moments in two specific scenes that I observed. The first pivotal moment happened when he was on a double date with his friend Bucky and two girls and he decided to take the offer to join the special project. He realized that the "special project" opportunity presented resonates with his own truth. The second was a remembering of his original "ah ha" moment. Captain America had become somewhat of a celebrity however he had not begun to serve the greater good in the way he knew he was created for. When soldiers were captured by Hydra, including his friend Bucky,

Cap broke orders and went on a rescue mission to save these men. He realized that his truth was to fight for freedom and righteousness, because entertaining soldiers on stage was not a part of his truth. Here another opportunity presented itself for Cap to utilize his new strengths and courage. The next moments after your "ah ha" is the time when you'll see yourself start to truly make better decisions, take risks, gain momentum, and build confidence for whatever you're doing or whoever you're becoming.

These moments of clarity are setup moments for the superhero, in you, who is soon to come. It is my belief that these clarifying moments are necessary to fine tune a better version of ourselves. There are things that we innately know about ourselves that we suppress because fear and doubt outweighs the confidence, and that fear is rooted deeply in the belief and value systems that were placed in us, whether intentionally or unintentionally, long ago.

An attribute shared by the superhero and the nemesis alike is that they have developed a remarkably high level of clarity of their self-awareness. Whether it is negative or positive, they mesh their self-awareness with their current state. They are highly aware of who they are at the present moment. Even when we see anti-heroes early on in some cases, we see their character as being conceited and prideful. There is a level of metacognition that is immediately apparent with the antihero that you barely see in the superhero and does not emerge until later in the story. Self-awareness plays a major role in the development of clarity in the character.

It is said, and backed by science, that our personalities are developed by the age of about eight. This means that up until this age, we are sponges and downloading everything we witness from our environment. Spanning from what we witness in our neighborhood, our friends, our schools and most importantly, what we witness in our family. This is a lot of information being absorbed and shaping our personality. This information, which is being absorbed, and sometimes incorrect, are programmed as belief systems in us as young children and builds our character. If the information is bad it will lead to incorrect belief systems and negative behavior. It is going to take reprogramming for your better self to emerge. The fortunate and unrealistic aspect for the superhero is that we see the complete reprogram almost instantly in the movies. In real life, however, it is a process and can sometimes take years before realizing there was incorrect information and beliefs and can take another few years to reprogram for a new healthier mind, body, and habit.

To delete the previous belief and value systems aka change the way you think and act, you will need to adopt and operate in a new belief and value system. These new systems absolutely have one purpose in mind. It is to make you better. What it entails is a lot of looking in the mirror, getting clarity on who you are now and who you want to become. It is to clearly see your strengths and weaknesses but to accept your weaknesses for what they are, just weaknesses. They are not hindrances. We all have weaknesses, whether they are flaws or just things that are not our strong suit. But a superhero accepts their weaknesses and will not let them hold or keep them from progressing ahead.

There is a belief system out there that tells people that they need to work on their weaknesses and build them up to strengths. Unless that weakness is rooted in fear and doubt and is a necessary part of your achievement and success, I believe this is one of the worst things you can follow. This system will have you concentrating and focusing on the weakness. This will have you view the weakness negatively and after a short period of time with no signs of improvement, you will view it as a waste of time which will negatively affect how you feel overall about your goal. You cannot improve a skill or become better by looking in that negative direction. If you are a college athlete and you're aspiring to play at the professional level but your weakness is telling jokes, then why would you work on learning how to deliver punch lines and improve your stage presence? This is a weakness that has nothing to do with you going to the professional sports level. This is a very extreme, off the wall scenario but I wanted to show how ridiculous it is to work on weaknesses when your focus should be on becoming great and improving the skills and talents you know you have and are needed. Working on weaknesses can be subtle as well. In past projects, I've focused countless hours on trying to create a brand logo knowing that I had an idea but didn't know how to make it a reality. It didn't become real until I was able to share my idea with someone who had the creation piece as their strength. It allowed me to focus on my true strength which was creating the material. Now I am not alluding to completely ignore your weaknesses. It depends on the role your weakness plays in your dream or desire. Let's take the same person who wants to play ball professionally. If a basketball player's weakness is the left side, then he/she absolutely must work on that to be a well-rounded and better player. The key is to make what you are good at great and what you are not so good at, better, if only what you are not good at is a part of the original desire.

Something to notice about superheroes is that they do not showcase their weaknesses, nor do they give attention to them, and they definitely do not allow themselves to be stopped by them. All they concentrate on is being the best superhero they can be. It is the reason people view their superhero as perfect; it is not that they do not have flaws and it's not that their weaknesses are masked. It's just not their focus and neither should your weakness be your focus. My favorite superhero is Batman because he is technically not "super". He doesn't have any superpowers or superhuman strength. However, he is very smart, highly creative, extraordinarily rich, and very innovative. These strengths and much more are what Batman highlights. So much so that you really cannot think of any weaknesses off the top of your head. Batman maximizes his strengths and abilities to their full potential. And when there is a weakness, if it plays a role in his crime fighting, he will then transform that weakness into a better strength without neglecting what he is great at. This gives him a clear picture of who he knows he is.

The same should go for you. Whatever you are striving to become, evaluate and test the belief and value systems that you have. These could be holding you back from being sucessful and great. If they are, you will need to start to make the necessary changes to adopt new belief and vaule systems that fit with you goal. What you will realize is that the systems and principles you start to place to make you into the superhero you want are identical to the systems, principles, routines, habits of every other superhero, successful person, celebrity, athlete who are considered great in their area of expertise.

CHAPTER III

The Character

One of the biggest excitements when a new superhero movie comes out is the unveiling of the costume or outfit. It's exciting because for those of us who have a memory of the old comic books or the old television shows and first-generation movies, that are now 30-40 years old, we now see how corny and lame those original costumes really were. No disrespect to those creators but they were limited in technology and based off the original comic books, not very innovative. The thrill now is to see what they have done with the old. How has it changed? How has it been upgraded? What new gadgets and hidden tricks does the new wardrobe house?

I remember a poll taken on social media about two different costumes for the first installment of the Wonder Woman movie. Gal Gadot ended up wearing the outfit that I did not vote for but still, the fact that they wanted the public's opinion was exciting, nonetheless. Iron Man is another one of my favorite characters, probably number two, for the same reasons as Batman. I was geeked about any movie he was in because I wanted to see what Tony Stark did to the Iron Man armor. What I loved most were the upgrades Tony Stark made each time. His Iron Man suit, still rather similar, had some changes as far as the look was concerned but the greatest difference was the evolution in its capabilities. It started with him having each individual piece "installed" on his person similar to an assembly line, to having small jet packs to fly across the room. He had his armor in a box. In one of the Avengers movies the hulk buster armor came down from orbit above the earth and he had a built-in helicopter suit. My personal favorite, the Nano-tech armor we saw in the last Avengers movie. His armor even crossed over to other superheroes as we saw the Nano-tech adapted for Spiderman and Pepper Potts.

There is something magical and esoteric about the different types of wardrobes that our favorite super beings have to adorn. What I have come to realize is that their costumes in so many ways reflect their character, not only as the super but also as the regular individual.

Superheroes have several strong character traits that make them whole and make us who watch adore them. They seemingly embody all that we feel is truly lacking within the world and quite possibly what is lacking within us which is why it is so easy for us to form a bond with those characters.

When we are first introduced to the character's alter ego, we see some of the heroic characteristics displayed in their actions & thoughts however it is almost always overshadowed by some type of fear and uncertainty. When we first get to know the character, we will laugh and mock because we know that the character is being portrayed to the extreme. We cannot possibly believe that there are people in the world that are this weak, meek, and clumsy. From our comfortable seats, we have all the answers, "stand up for yourself, why don't they do this, why didn't they just say it?" We have the answers however the same conflicts we see on the screen are brewing all around us. It is in our family members, in our friends, in our children and it is in our own lives, but most people do not recognize or the recognition is short lived in real life. People definitely do not want to acknowledge it in real life.

The first conflict they encounter is usually a testament to their true character. It is the truth they believe or the righteousness that they stand for that gets them in trouble or beat up however these standards are unwavering. It is just that they are lacking physical strength and confidence to support them against a bully. These character traits first witnessed are what are going to collectively set the foundation of the superhero we will soon see.

So, back to the question. Are superheroes born or created? Again, my answer is that they are developed. If they are developed, does that mean anyone can be a superhero? Absolutely yes! A superhero can be developed at any age, any gender, any ethnicity, any education, or financial level.

It takes a mindset shift, heart shift, development of skills, and a change to the "attire", we will explore these, to develop into a superhero. We know the costume is the thing that really showcases the superhero and is enjoyed by millions of kids and adults alike every year on October 31st.

Of course, all superheroes have flaws, they are not perfect even though we want them to be. The key to building a superhero is to realize the best traits, develop them, live by them every day, and apply them to every situation. This is one of the things that makes them so fascinating. Their ability to focus on being the best version of themselves. They live out their best selves, no matter the role or task. Unlike those who focus on and try to emulate others without going through the process of development.

How do you build you a superhero? Good question, I'm glad you asked. Let me show you the basic ingredients.

CHAPTER IV

The Belt

Attribute of Truth

The first item that goes into building a superhero is the belt. Every superhero needs a belt, and most do have one in one form or another. As I stated before, my favorite superhero is Batman and I love the fact that he does not have superpowers. One thing he does have is that he is respected and admired by his fellow superhero friends and feared by his enemies. And boy oh boy, does he have one helluva belt! His utility belt is one of the most reliable items in his arsenal. It also has several capabilities but serves one purpose, it contains almost anything he needs for almost any situation.

Today people wear a belt as strictly a fashion accessory, others wear them as a functional fashion accessory, some wear for functional purposes only and plenty of others do not wear one at all... by choice! Personally, I cannot wear any type of pants or shorts without a belt unless it is sweatpants or athletic shorts, even with those I still need a drawstring. The purpose of the belt is to anchor and stabilize your attire and keep your pants from falling and showing your ass, that is literal and figurative. It keeps your shirt tucked and prevents exposing your skin and undergarments. Thousands of years ago, during war time, the belt held the soldier's armor together. It also served as a utility belt to hold the weapons or the tools of war. And today, the belt serves the same purpose for soldiers and law enforcement.

The reason why I wanted to talk about the belt as the first piece of the costume to building a superhero is because of the stability and centering the belt provides. The belt is the characteristic of absolute truth. Truth by definition is the quality or state of being true. However, truth can be distorted by one's perspective and experiences. A child can grow up and have his/her own perspective of how they are to raise their own family. They have a truth and it is valid in their own eyes. The issue is what the standard that their truth is being held against.

Absolute truth is the standard to be measured against. The absolute truth is unwavering. Now if we take the same scenario of the young child, make it a bit more specific and measure it against absolute truth, we get different perspectives of truth. If they were raised in a household where a parent was always drinking, getting drunk and using obscene language, they could grow up to never drink, never get drunk and never curse because they learned & understood that there's an absolute truth. This child learned along the way that drinking, getting drunk and using foul language was not right and true and is never right or true. There was a standard that they learned. They were able to compare their experience against the standard and learned that what he/she grew up in as "normal" was not normal, nor a standard of absolute truth.

All superheroes have a "what" and a "why" for their purpose. Their what and why is made up of two components. One of the components is their truth. It is their "non-compete clause" that cannot be compromised. It is the reason they will live, fight, and die for. Their truth can and will be measured against absolute truth. When it is, there is not much difference between the absolute truth and their truth. Having a truth that can be measured against and aligned with absolute truth is one of the foundations of building a superhero.

One reason for needing a solid foundation of truth is because the belief and value systems that we have could be corrupted. We have no control over how our origin story begins. As I alluded to previously, our personalities are not developed until around the age of eight, give or take a year or two. Our environment up until this age is writing a lot of our story. In order to develop our truth, there are three things we need to know. First point, we have to know our origin story. There is truth to the old saying "in order to know where we're going, we have to know where we come from". This is important for point three. Second point, we have to understand our origin stories. Understanding our origin is key because there are aspects in our past that we need to understand why they happened the way that they did. There could be some buried hurt and pain that we only understand through our own perspective which is usually a myopic viewpoint. There needs to be an understanding from other perspectives. The third point is that we need to be aware and be sure that we are not currently expressing any negative and corrupt actions or feelings that are rooted in the incorrect belief and value systems from our origin story. This is why we need to know our origin story. These three points open the door for two things, understanding that we are able to forgive what took place in the past and gives way to a deeper realization of one's true self. Being able to tell the difference between your past belief systems, which are rooted in corrupt values, and actual truth about your potential to be heroic is what serves as your belt. This is the start to building your best and true self, your superhero self.

At the end of this book, there is a chance to sketch, build, and mold your superhero. Take a moment to think about the truth that you want your superhero character to have. More importantly, think about what your truth currently says? Is it a product of your origin story or has it been developed to represent your true and best self?

As you begin to understand the false beliefs that were ingrained as truths and overcome the emotional hurts that stunted you from becoming the superhero of your life, you will begin to see the reality that you can actually become a superhero. You'll also realize that you've always had the ability to become a superhero. The window you were looking through was actually a painting which blocked you from seeing outside and blocked you from knowing that there was an outside. Ed Mylett says "Everything happens for you, not to you". I love this quote. The value I draw from this phrase is that every superhero needs a nemesis. The journey to becoming super heroic needs opposition and tragedy. The archenemy, your archenemy, enhances the epic triumph and makes victory that much sweeter and the journey worth watching.

CHAPTER V

The Symbol

Attribute of Virtue and Righteousness

Ahhhh! This is where some imagination and creativity can come into play. The time where we can be children again. I have two boys and they would love to imagine and create their own superhero costumes. Is it me or do all kids have the same core costume? Their cape, made from a towel or coat. Daddy's work gloves that are way too big. A mask made of a t-shirt or a dress sock. A weapon that is some piece of house equipment, whether a plunger, large utensil, or something that can cause pain or damage to a wall. We know for a fact that someone or something will get hit. And that's it. Absolutely nothing else because almost all kids, including you and I, put on our superhero outfit with no pants on, just "tighty whitey's". You cannot help but fall in love with children's imagination. The one thing that stands out from the rest of the outfit is what they choose as their symbol or the representation of their superhero. Some will choose a symbol from a well-known superhero but many others will choose to come up with their own symbol that represents their own superhero. The symbol is the mark. Probably the most famous is the very well-known 'S' on the chest. For a child's costume, this is normally their favorite t-shirt that has the picture of something that they cherish. This symbol can have a life of its own, its own personality and it directs our little superhero in all that they will do.

Quick story, at about 18 months old, our oldest son knew how to put on his favorite DVD movies, hit play, start the movie and replay over and over. If we had let him, he could watch either Finding Nemo or Jurassic Park three times in a row. Excuse our parenting but it did happen once. By the age of three, his fascination with dinosaurs had grown. He loved anything and everything dinosaur, from the purple one that sang and danced to the giant ones seen in the movies. What supported his dinosaur obsession even more is that at restaurants, he would order a side salad or broccoli to go with his meals while most other kids would order fries. His favorite color was green at the time as well so there you go.

I remember there were two dinosaur t-shirts that he wanted to wear every day. One was a dark blue that had multiple dinosaurs on them with their names and he was going to be the superhero that saved all the dinosaurs from the asteroid. Often, he would randomly take on the personality of one of the dinos on his shirt. When he was T-Rex, it meant that it was time to take something out and that usually meant I was in for it and I needed to watch my back. The point I was making before I took a memory lane detour is that the symbol, which is normally front and center of the chest, is the second component of the 'what and why' mentioned previously. This symbol is a reminder of the superheroes reason and willingness to live, fight, and even die for. It is usually placed on the chest near the heart because what is in the heart is represented by the symbol and the symbol is reflected in the heart. It is the moral compass and the sole purpose of virtue and righteousness.

Unfortunately, we live in a world that has become more and more rooted in 'opinionated judgement' and commentary. Social media is being abused as an outlet for individual opinions to be the measuring stick for judgement. A good majority feel that their opinions are the facts, the law, absolute and are the only valid source of truth and righteousness. Anything that goes against their opinion will be judged, unfriended, blocked, banned, and unfortunately killed. This world is in major need of superheroes. More today than ever before.

Just like truth, virtue and righteousness can be skewed by one's experiences. Let's face it, we all know the difference between right and wrong. That is not hard to figure out at all. If it were about right versus wrong, this world would be in a better moral state. The majority does not want to purposely be bad or evil. Most who do perpetrate bad or evil actions are usually doing it out of lack or desperation and continue as a means of satisfying emotional connection to the lack. This is just my opinion from observing the villains.

There are two Bible verses that say, "each man did what was right in his own eyes and there is a way that seems right to a man but in the end is death". That means that in their hearts and minds, they were convinced that what they were doing was right. Even worse it means that there was nothing present in their life to measure the decision making against that told them that they were wrong. The overarching theme from those Bible verses was that everyone acted according to their own personal standards, personal beliefs, feelings, emotions, happiness and hurt. (Interjecting that when I say righteousness I do not mean in the religious sense of the word. Doing something right according to the law or kindness is righteousness. Crossing a street at the crosswalk is righteousness while jay walking is not.) Fast forward through history and we see the only difference between now and those times is that technology has advanced but people are still the same. There is no absolute virtue and righteousness to be measured against, there is no standard. This has been the norm for a very long time with fantasy superheroes now filling the role as virtuous & righteous filled leaders. So, the issue then is not right vs wrong but right vs almost right. Then the question is, what is right? And what is the standard for righteousness and virtue?

Like truth, absolute righteousness and virtue are unwavering, and to be unwavering, there needs to be a standard set in place. If I can take the earlier example of the child growing up with an alcoholic parent. When they became an adult, they decided not to repeat the same actions they saw as a child. Now an opposite scenario can apply as well. Another child in the same household can grow up and repeat all of the same behavior they've witnessed from the parent. Their justification would be that they feel those negative actions and abusive behavior is how it is supposed to be. They've convinced themselves that it was normal and right behavior because that is how it's always been. The difference between the two children is the standards that they set up in each of their lives as adults. One child believed that the behavior was not of virtue nor of righteousness and that their symbolic representation of parenting was going to be lived as one of virtue and righteousness. They also learned that the insults hurled at them as a child were completely wrong and was not going to set the standard for their life. Another major aspect is one sibling's willingness to change the narrative of iniquity and foulness to virtuous and right.

The virtues and righteousness that go into building your superhero self will be those that represent the best of yourself. These traits will not only be admired by others but should inspire others as well. Since we are building ourselves into a superhero, some necessary virtues are courage, fortitude, self-control, love, caring,

Approachable	Appreciative	Balanced
Disciplined	Ethical	Faithful
Loving	Moral	Objective

honesty and inquisitive just to name a few. What character traits or virtues do you want to couple with your truth that will serve as the foundation of your superhero? One attribute to consider is that when you become a superhero, servitude is your greatest responsibility. The second greatest responsibility will be growth. Some of the greatest superheroes of life embody these two traits, a desire to serve others and a desire for personal improvement and development. You will find that superheroes grow and learn more in order to serve the citizens of their city. The virtues we choose are the ones we have to aspire to in order to become a superhero, not only for ourselves but for the world around us. Positive virtues and righteous actions are the backbone to living a life full of heroism.

Here's a small list of some positive attributes to consider while building your superhero. Write down any and all positive attributes that you do not see that you would like to see in your superhero. It's my hope that you get to see yourself for possibly the first time and realize greatness in you. It is hard to think about this if it's your first time. If you are having difficulty, please by all means draw virtues from your favorite superheroes.

Calm	Confident	Courageous	Dedicated
Fun	Genuine	Honest	Logical
Selfless	Stable	Trusting	Wise

CHAPTER VI

The Shoes

Attribute of Peace

Peace is a daily, a weekly, a monthly process, gradually changing opinions, slowly eroding old barriers, quietly building new structures – John F Kennedy

I am no stranger to being in situations where the atmosphere got hostile and chaotic, as we all have experienced. I have also held positions where the day to day tasks were a bit intense. I used to state that I love that type of atmosphere because that is where my nature always shined brightest since I have a strong but calm nature, and I try to think logically first and not respond based on emotions. I am a person who can think and respond rationally in almost any situation. However, there are times that I remember vividly when the chaos/hostility affected me deeply and I felt incompetent and unworthy. The reason why the chaos affected me in those moments was I let it disturb my inner peace. Having peace, inner peace, mental peace, a peaceful spirit is built by a series of habits. Having peace will direct your decision making and have confidence in those decisions, influence the way you live your life, and give you a high level of clarity.

This leads to another necessary part of the building of the superhero, the shoes. The running, jumping, landing, kicking, skidding. Doing all the evil fighting and galaxy saving that superheroes do, it has to be about the shoes and careful consideration goes into them. Mostly everyone has a few pairs of shoes for various occasions. You are not going to wear your black leather dress shoes to the beach, and you will not wear your beach sandals to a formal event. What you wear on your feet needs to fit the reason for wearing them.

The shoes of the superhero must have a number of aspects to them. They must be comfortable, durable, and functional which will provide the superhero with peace and clarity. The right shoes ensure a stable footing and can help increase confidence in their movement. Having on the wrong shoes for a specific occasion can almost guarantee a level of embarrassment and stress. Having a peaceful presence is an aspect greatly admired and helps keep the person focused and calm. Let's face it, one thing you do not see superheroes do is trip over loose laces or wear the wrong shoes. Also, what can seem oxymoronic is that in any given situation, your superhero can still perform even in the wrong shoes. Why? Because they have a level of peace that surpasses all understanding.

Just like truth, righteousness, and virtue there is absolute peace and there is a false sense of peace. Absolute peace only comes in one form however a false sense of peace comes in many forms. I call it a false sense of peace for two reasons: 1) it is temporary 2) the outlet used to garner peace is usually tied to a negative habit.

There are positive and constructive habits that bring about peace and are tied to a person who has a high level of self-awareness and emotional intelligence. This person knows how to achieve absolute peace during chaos and this outlet is usually to spark an idea or resolution to the challenge or problem.

Since we're building a superhero, this is for one who is having trouble with establishing true and absolute peace in their life. The person I'm talking about is the one who allows the anger, frustration, confusion and trouble to turn into worry, panic and anxiety and then uses alcohol, sex, prescription medication, illicit drugs, excessive & unnecessary shopping, avoidance, doubt and a host of other outlets as their gateway to peace. These all provide a false sense of peace because 1) they are temporary and not true fixes and 2) they are negative and unhealthy responses. They do not eliminate the worry and anxiety and if left unresolved, they can lead to another destructive or worse behavior. Our beloved superheroes have had to overcome this same obstacle. They realized that in order to be great, a removal of any viruses and blockages of peace were a necessity. Some of the greatest moments in a hero's life is when they were able to overcome what has been holding them back from being their best. They understood that heroism and peace need to travel together because any rival can show up at any time and allow chaos to cause life to fall apart.

Obtaining absolute peace produces rest, calm, tranquility, stability and most of the time answers to issues, in the face of the problem. To have absolute peace you need to live out your life with a series of good, healthy habits that fall in line with your truth, virtues and righteousness. For example, if you are always around someone who is angry, you can do two things. You can steer away from the chronically angry people or, if compassion is one of the attributes you listed, you can try developing a habit of listening first, listen for the true issue, understanding the situation or state of mind and offering a friendly ear and/or a calm word of advice. The root of that anger is usually wrapped up in a hurt that has not been resolved and your compassion and inner peace just may be the resolution that they are looking for. Your peaceful presence just may calm the storm.

The shoes are so important because they are symbolic of how the superhero lives out their life and how they handle issues in a peaceful manner, with a peace of mind and a sound heart. It is a series of habits performed each day and in each situation that build a solid foundation and stable footing for them to live by. Superheroes also know that absolute peace cannot be acted out physically until it is manifested internally. True peace starts with calm in the mind, heart, soul, spirit first and an understanding of how to apply it before it can be expressed towards others. Peace is practiced.

Taking the angry person mentioned above. If they desire peace and want to make a true change and get a better hold of their anger, they must implement some new thoughts about themselves, operate in different belief systems, and perform different actions than before. In addition, and just as important, they need to elevate their EQ (emotional intelligence). They're going to have to also dig deep within themselves and uncover the root reason for their ill-temperedness.

One superhero that comes to mind that epitomizes this is Captain America. Captain Rodgers screamed peace. The only times I have seen him chaotic was in his memory flashback. However, he was bringing about his inner peace by performing his habit of taking out the pain on the heavy bags. This was building and ensuring his foundation so that when real chaos comes, like his famous elevator fight, he will have clarity and peace to face anything that comes his way.

It may sound strange but peace, inner peace, peace of mind and a sound heart has its roots in the shoes that are worn. Your peace will come from strong habits that you build and live out, how you "walk" in life. These habits should improve your physical, mental, and emotional health. They should be the regulator and filter of the items that are allowed into your body, whether by hearing, sight, consumption, or atmosphere. A real-life example is Robert Downey, Jr who famously plays Iron Man. He took up the martial art Wing Chun as one of his habits to bring about peace in his personal life. There are certain things that a superhero will not compromise on and neither should you if you want to become a superhero. To have peace ultimately means you must be a peacemaker. Being a peacemaker means you bring about peace by going to war, literally and figuratively. The next three items of a superhero's makeup are designed for just that.

CHAPTER VII

The Shield

Attribute of Faith

Every single characteristic listed previously is essential. They need to be a part of every person's character no matter what, whether they are a superhero, want to be a superhero or just want to be a good person. These attributes are always necessary characteristics and should be on display at all times.

To better illustrate this, we can look at a defensive football player. They play the same game as their offensive counterpart however they study and play the game from a different perspective. They do not handle the football constantly, but they do need to know how to handle the football if they should come into possession of it. The offensive team practices throwing, catching, running and throwing routes, and although this is not the main focus for the defensive player, they need to know how to handle, protect, and run the ball should they need to recover a fumble or an interception. The cornerbacks focus is to prevent the receiver from catching the ball. In the event of the receiver catching the ball, the corner is supposed to stop the receiver from gaining more yardage. The actual handling of the football is not a cornerback's main responsibility; however, he needs to know how to handle the football in case he forces a turnover. It is still very necessary and key to be an effective defensive player.

Just like the defensive football player, these next set of attributes are very important to have but are not required to use all the time. These are specifically for use in times of trouble. Of the next characteristics, there is one I believe to be the most essential.

The trust system is the foundation of the next set of character traits and at the core of the actions you take and the decisions you make. It acts as a deterrent for things to avoid for your life and a passageway for what to accept. Whether for the positive or negative, from a state of wisdom or ignorance, faith and what you have it grounded in will govern how you live your life. Faith is your shield of protection.

When we look at the superhero world, we see a lot of them have some type of shield of protection. Wonder Woman has her shield & arm bands, The Green Lanterns have their rings, The Hulk has his thick skin, Iron Man has his suit of armor and of course Captain America has his famous shield. All significantly different but they serve the same purpose. Protection. It is the faith in this protection that the superhero relies on to keep them safe.

Something very key to mention here that is very important to this characteristic and the characteristics to follow is that in order for them to be effective, they have to be in use. You see, Cap's shield is not always in use. When not in use, it does not prevent him from being Cap. However, when Cap needs to use his trusty shield, it performs as he expects it and it performs exactly how he uses it. The key is that the shield must always be available and put into action when necessary.

Every new year millions of people around the world make faith promises, resolutions, to themselves and within a short amount of time, many of those faith promises are broken and stopped, until the next new year. Why that is so is because at the first sign of trouble or temptation, their trust in the promise they made themselves is not as strong as hoped. The ones who do have faith and endure end up making incredibly positive and drastic changes to their life.

Since I am comparing the shield to faith, we all know what a shield is but what is faith and how is it protection? Faith simply put is complete trust. It is also complete confidence that something is real or going to happen although it hasn't happened yet. Many of us have experienced our pet dog running away and this is especially traumatizing for a child. The fear and anxiety that sets in because of the unknown whereabouts of the dog is very unsettling. Our faith, when activated, steps in and protects. Although a child and their family do not know the whereabouts of their beloved dog, they do have faith that the dog will be returned home safely. Part of the activation of faith takes place when the family goes and looks for the dog around the neighborhood, posts signs and asks the neighbors for help. When that faith is strong, it protects them from having any negative thoughts about their dog's fate. It also protects them from accepting a reality that may not be true. Again, faith will act as a deterrent for what to avoid especially when it negatively attacks your mental & emotional wellbeing.

Faith must be looked at as the shield that protects you from the shots fired from weapons of those things that don't want the best for you. Just as important, faith will also protect you from those who care for you who will say they are doing what they do to "protect" you. Most of the time, those words of love are coming from a place of his/her hurt and pain. Your faith also becomes your shield in this situation because it can protect you from negativity, doubt, fear, discouragement, and uncertainty. What you need to realize as well is that these will not always come from outside sources. Your shield will also have to protect you from your own negative thoughts, which are rooted in the corrupted belief and value systems that you are changing. I'm compelled to make you aware that the most frequent opposition comes from yourself and usually takes the longest to change. The good thing is that the shield of faith is specifically designed to protect you from external as well as internal thoughts, negativity or opposition. It reinforces the reason why you're on the journey to developing a superhero in the first place.

Benefits of trusting in the protection of your shield is it allows you to fully concentrate on being influential, effective, and the best superhero you can be without worrying about 'what ifs'. The biggest superheroes, even the real ones, trust in the faith of who they are and only focus on making the greatest positive impact in his/her community and in the world.

I saw this played out in two movies, Captain America: Winter Soldier and the final fight scene of Avengers: Endgame. In Winter Soldier, after the great fight scene in the elevator, Cap is faced with the decision of jumping out of the elevator and falling about 20 stories below. His decision took a mere second and then he leaps, having faith that his shield will protect him. It did, he landed safely, got up and started running.

In Endgame, Thanos is fighting Thor and right before Thor is about to meet his fate, Thanos gets hit by Thor's hammer. Captain America is the one who is wielding the hammer. Yeah, the movie audience screamed with excitement. The fight between Cap and Thanos ramps back up and Cap takes a serious beating while his famous shield is close to broken in half. Now, most of us with half a shield would have abandoned the shield and continued the fight with just the weapon(s) and our skillset to fight. Not Captain America, he gets back up and retightens his half-broken shield to his arm. This showed he still had 100% trust and confidence in his shield, and he was determined to still use his faith. This shield, along with his new weapon, he decided to keep fighting against Thanos.

As you are building your superhero, your faith will have to be coupled with determination, perseverance, and sheer will against all opposing forces. Here is the great tell that your faith is working when it's coupled with these aspects, you will get help along the way. Access to resources will show up unexpectedly. You may have hoped for them, but it is your action that allowed those resources to show up and come alongside you. In the movie, all the "snapped" superheroes show back up. Now that's what I call a confidence booster and faith builder!

If it was never apparent before, it was definitely apparent in that scene. Cap displayed true leadership through his trust. What he did is what I want to encourage in you, refrain from the evil forces of fear, self-doubt, past and current disappointments. Instead muster up courage, the will to keep going, and the strength to see your journey through to the end. Faith, trust, perseverance, determination, and will all catapult you up the ladder to the Superhero hall of fame.

CHAPTER VIII

The Helmet

Attribute of a Strong Mindset

The helmet! This part of the super's costume is probably my favorite for two reasons. One, it was created to protect the head, the most important part of the body in my eyes and two, pardon my French when I say this but because the helmets are just badass. There have been some cool looking helmets around the superhero universe, but my favorite helmet is not even related to superheroes. It is the Spartan helmet from the movie 300. I do not want to say it again, but I will, those helmets are straight-up badass. Now that I think about it, I need to get one in my life.

You might argue about what the most important part of the hero's construct is and that is ok because what is more important to you is a testament to your truth. In my opinion, it's the helmet because of what it protects. It is so important that it is not just for superheroes. They are worn in sports, in construction, in transportation, in underground mining, and in the military. The helmet is structurally designed to prevent/reduce significant risk of injury to the head and/or neck. Given the nature of the work of superheroes and any person in the above-mentioned professions, a well-designed and equipped helmet is a necessity.

How To Build A Superhero

In recent years, the cinema industry has highlighted a few superheroes with great helmets. Iron Man has had the best with the advanced technology and top-notch capabilities. Paired with all that is going on in the mind of Tony Stark, of course his head needs the best protection his money and intelligence can buy.

Without a question or doubt, the brain is the most vital organ in the body. It's the control center and in the superhero world, it would be headquarters. Here's why it's so important. If an individual has a heart attack, they may still have a decent quality of life with a damaged heart. If there is a loss limb, the medical industry has made great strides with advancements in prosthetics. Brain damage however, dependent on the area of injury, can tremendously reduce the quality of life. Brain injuries can induce coma's, impair motor and cognitive functions, as well as impair the senses. There's a greater handicap risk with a brain injury. Brain injuries are exceedingly difficult to recover and heal from.

In my honest opinion, what could be considered more traumatic than a brain injury is a mind that is stagnant and is purposely not being utilized to its fullest potential. This is an even greater handicap because it can last a lifetime in a person who has not suffered any physical injury. This type of mindset could possibly be rooted in a past emotional or mental injury as a result of the old corrupt belief and value system. I am no scientist or doctor but from what I have read and studied, the brain is the only organ that can literally change and become a different brain than it was before. No, it will not change its shape, but the elasticity and synapses can change and form new connections by way of new experiences, new habits and new thought processing. These reasons, as well as many, many others are why a helmet is so vital. It is because it protects the source of power (the brain and the mindset) of the superhero.

We love when our superheroes band together to fight against a big enemy and we genuinely appreciate their ability to stand alone too. We admire their individuality. The superhero mindset is the source for why they are who they are. It is the source of their personality, their creativity, their perception, their thinking, their awareness, their perseverance, their dignity, their strong will just to name a few. It makes up who they are and is one of the reasons why we have our favorites. We feel like we bond with our favorite superhero because we know their back story. In many cases they were not always the courageous one and we know that they were a bit quirky and weird. Some were overzealous and conceited; however, we now know they all needed some development and refinement.

The important thing to know is that to fulfill the superhero inside you, you must go through a transformation. You must change in some way. I always say that the word "change" is the most hated word in the world, in any language, however it is the most important and the most necessary. All changes have their start in the mind. To activate your faith, you must start with your mind. Value, worth, absolute truth, and wisdom all connect with the mind. Each superhero had to go through this and the person that came out on the other side is the one we most admire.

A strong mindset is only a piece of the puzzle. For a superhero to be optimal, their mindset (Helmet) and virtues (Symbol), which represents the heart & emotions, must work together. Your perception of the outside world dictates how you operate in it. Your perception can be influenced by your mindset and the health of your emotions. Having a weak mindset coupled with good virtues do not allow you to perform optimally to be your best superhero self. Vice versa does not work well either. It's a setup that leads to abandoning the journey to building a superhero. During this process of transformation heroes had to accept some truths about themselves and do away with the inaccuracies they thought were the truth. They had to change their thinking, remove the negative and build on the positive. They also had to change their virtues, belief systems, and up their emotional intelligence. Changing all of this is not just about getting rid of the negative but it is also about increasing and stacking on the positive and healthy. In order to be a superhero they had to change the way that they viewed and perceived reality. And this, I believe, is just the beginning of going from ordinary to extraordinary. This is a lifelong process of development for their character. In the Marvel cinematic universe, we see the evolution of Tony Starks' Ironman suits. The suits evolved as Tony Stark himself also evolved. In the beginning his suit was made of solid metal, but by the end in the last Avengers movie, his suit is made of nanotechnology. In the same way, mindsets, emotional intelligence and virtues also need to evolve.

So, what type of helmet/protection is needed to become a superhero? We cannot walk around in our daily lives wearing an actual helmet, unless we work in construction, play sports or ride motorcycles, but we can fortify our minds so that we have an extraordinarily strong mindset. To have a strong mindset, we need to have a healthy mind and a healthy way of thinking.

A healthy mind needs healthy nutrition. That nutrition will come in two forms. One from the actual nutrients that are being consumed from food and the second from what is being consumed through what you see, hear, read, and think. With all the "mishegas" going on that is coming through almost every device we watch, voices that we hear, and words we read, it is no wonder that most people live life in fear or anger. If you can control what your mind consumes, you can create a superhero mindset. Evolving into a superhero's mindset must be developed. Some ways to do so is by reading positive, self-development material, listening to mind nourishing material in podcasts and music. One habit I've developed in my personal development is that each morning I visualize putting on my helmet to protect my mind. That's done through meditation, reading, exercise, and learning. And with each item I complete, I can picture myself adding another piece of protection to protect my creative and precious mind. Once you begin to elevate your mindset as well as raise and secure your emotional intelligence, you'll begin to build new belief and value systems but the true benefit is that you'll elevate to superhero status and become legendary.

CHAPTER IX

The Weapon

Gifts, Talents, and Abilities

Out of all the things that make up a superhero, the majority believes that this is everyone's favorite part of the superhero's persona. The weapons and really cool gadgets. It does not matter how old you are, we all have a favorite superhero and we know exactly what his/her weapon or special ability is and how it is used. I think we are all able to identify with one superhero or two. When growing up we have dreamed about getting the weapon for Christmas or our birthday. Then when we got it, Boy O Boy, we slept with the weapon, bathed with our weapon, and practiced our special abilities. You know the special abilities like flipping over the back of the sofa or sneaking up on parents and siblings and testing how strong we were and proving how weak they are. Some of us now get to relive this fun with our own children especially since superhero movies and television shows have resurged after going through some major reboots over the last few decades.

As I stated earlier, each one of these latter attributes must be put into action and utilized to be effective. That is ever so true with the weapons and abilities of our superheroes. I mean, for the most part, this is just another great reason why we adore them. For the umpteenth time, Batman is my favorite superhero. Ordinary dude with no special powers but his talents and abilities are extraordinary. His weapons and vehicles, even more extraordinary. And I guess it helps that he's a billionaire. I think I should throw that minor detail in there too. The weapon is different from the rest of the items in building a superhero. It is the only piece that is specifically used for the offensive and should not be sitting on the shelf collecting dust. All of the other parts that we have talked about is about fortifying and protecting the superhero. They are the "glue" that holds the purpose together for the fight. The weapon on the other hand, is for the fight.

Putting on a superhero suit is easy. We can have the helmet on our head, the emblem shining bright on our chest, and the shoes on our feet. We can look good standing outside under the bright sun; however, it is all useless and means nothing if there is not a valid reason that calls for a superhero and if there are no talents, abilities, and gifts ready to be used for battle.

The abilities we have showcase what we can do and why we are important and the potential value we can offer to the world. They allow us to move out of the realm of mediocrity and into the realm of potential. When we progressively develop our talents, abilities and gifts and partner them with a strong mindset, truth, virtue, & righteousness, they fit hand in hand and step us into the realm of infinite potential. They all go together like a slice of cake and glass of milk, wings and blue cheese, left jab, and right uppercut. When you see all of your superhero's aspects work together to defeat a foe, you feel an adrenaline rush and a strong sense of accomplishment and achievement. Why? Because you identify with that superhero. That hero embodies your true beliefs and values. You also become emotionally connected. We then become envious in a good way. Just think of how great that feeling is when you embody your superhero yourself and accomplish your dreams and goals in a heroic way. You can imagine yourself in that outfit, flying, performing powerful kicks and punches, throwing one of the villains' goons through a brick wall. You can picture yourself in that fight kicking serious butt. But the unfortunate part is that most people leave the fighting ability to the fantasy world of the movie or comic book. After the movie ends, they return to lives that are mediocre or of not much value. They continue repeating negative and self-doubting mantras about themselves. They continue believing that they are less than and will never be like the superhero they admire. Words like 'I wish I were brave like' or 'I will never be as strong as' become a broken record in their thoughts. This type of self-talk leads to a life unfulfilled and possible depression. Let's face it, most superheroes are at this point in their origin story when they first discover their superpowers and realize that their lives are meant for more than what they have been used for.

This is normally the story of everyone who is great and one of the reasons why most people do not live to their full potential. The experiences of life have left most people in a state of feeling less than and they've forgotten their true selves. Les Brown is quoted as saying 'the wealthiest place on the planet is the graveyard'. Why? Because there were an innumerable number of brilliant minds, untapped potential, and unused talents and abilities that never got to see the light of day. Those resources that never got to be or were lost way too early could have been the revolutionary answer to some problem that we are still living with today.

My wife and I experienced a miscarriage extremely late in the pregnancy of our would be second son. Just a few weeks from the expected due date. I do wonder sometimes who he would have become. What greatness was inside him that would have changed the world. It was an extremely complicated pregnancy and the miscarriage left my wife and I emotionally and mentally torn. About five months later we were blessed and overly joyed with news that another son would soon be born to us. There is no doubt in my mind that he would have been great, however, the two sons we are blessed to raise now is where our concentration is placed. If either my wife or I were to still be emotionally or mentally concentrated on the miscarriage, we would seriously neglect and miss the benefits of being able to raise the two lives right in front of us. Too many people neglect their present and hide their talents because of focusing on their past. Something that was said or something that has happened has led them to believe that they cannot be significant because of it. If you know that you're doing it right now, I beg you to stop delaying the expression of your gifts and talents.

This is the bigger issue that lies with the people today. They're either too busy, too scared, too submissive to fear or the past, and/or too doubtful to want to be a better self. Let alone a superhero. There are people with talents and abilities that are absolute gifts, however their mindset is that they are not good enough, in some way, to showcase it to the world. Their mind tells them that there are others who are better or deserve success more and their hearts say to stay right where they are and watch others enjoy life through their abilities instead. They think too heavily on the negative 'what if's'. What if you think of the positive 'what if's'? What if you do succeed? What if someone likes it? What if you end up helping a dire situation? Thinking on the positive what ifs can lead to positive affirmations which can develop into positive incantations. Now your self-talk will change to "I will succeed", "someone will like it", "I have the necessary skills". If you are afraid to fail, you are afraid to succeed. If you believe, trust, and put into action, it will give you a boost in confidence to not only get started but allows you to follow through. And over time, you will increase, grow, and elevate. This is how mindset, valuable belief systems and abilities work hand in hand. The helmet that represents mindset, the weapon that represents your talents, gifts, & abilities, the shield that represents faith, the belt that represents your inner truth, and the symbol that represents your heart & belief systems all coupled with commitment and a strong desire & work ethic are the major building blocks for creating a superhero that can save the world.

The graveyard may be wealthy but above ground is much wealthier. Above ground has more value. If you are reading this, guess what, you're above ground and you are valuable. What you possess is more valuable than you may realize but it will never be realized if you do not explore what is inside you. It does not matter how old or how young, how tall or how short, all you need to know is if the weapon is in your hand, is it being utilized? How well do you know your weapon? Know yourself, understand yourself. Whatever has you chained to a prison that prevents your glorious self needs to be broken. The chains need to come off and in most cases the chains are not tied to a foundation. Do not neglect your talents, abilities, and gifts. When they are neglected and forgotten, it just leads to a life full of pain and curses. Trust me when I tell you, you are more capable than you realize. Whatever you have, Develop it! Use it!

Each one of us are born an original with unique abilities and talents. These unique weapons that we possess are supposed to be used to their fullest potential to bring about good in the world. Someone needs to be rescued, taught, and encouraged by you. Someone needs their inner superhero to be realized. Whether you have multiple weapons like Batman or Black Widow or just one like Thor, your talents and abilities are supposed to be uncovered, developed, utilized, and unleashed. Not just for the fulfillment of your life but for the betterment of others. These two pieces of your outfit, the helmet, and the weapon share something great – they are the representation of the unlimited power inside of you. A strong mindset and talents, gifts, and abilities all house great power. Unleash it! Postpone no more!

CHAPTER X

The Communication

Importance of Effective Communication

Earlier I stated that a healthy mind comes from healthy nutrition in two forms. The second form is by what we hear, see, read, and think. That is summed up as effective communication. Communication can either cause the greatest downfall or be the greatest building block. If you don't believe me, ask any failed relationship, whether business or personal, or even worse, ask the survivors of a military assault where a lack of communication played a part or communications failed.

Whenever there is war, one of the first offensive strategies is to take out the communications of the opposition. If communication can be disrupted, then confusion can occur between the troops and their command. This allows the opposition to have an advantage and exploit the disconnect. Poor or lack of communication can lead to death, but effective, positive communication can lead to great success.

Superheroes have a huge load on their shoulders. Keeping the world and the universe safe is a heavy lift. This responsibility requires that they effectively communicate. You and I, as well, no matter our jobs, responsibilities, or relationships we need to learn to communicate clearly and concisely, to do our job to the best of our ability.

There are basic components that make communication effective. Clarity, conciseness, responsibility, and trust to name a few. I want to first get into it quickly, for the sake of being a superhero, having effective communication is highly dependent on having the right people around you. Having the right people who all have a single source of their absolute truth that can be depended on to relay the best and most accurate information is key to a successful superhero life. Superheroes do not have all the answers. Some of the answers they do have could be wrong. Although each superhero is great on their own, what makes them even more extraordinary is the fact that they have a supportive team of the right people telling them exactly what they need to hear. Although they may not want to hear what is being told. This is what it means to have a best friend or an accountability partner. They are on your side 100% and they should also tell you the truth about yourself when you get out of line. I have a large group of accountability partners who I consider brothers. One of them said this to me when we were discussing accountability in one of our meetings. He said we need to be able to tell each other "your slip is showing". Basically, that means that you are exposing a part of yourself that shouldn't and needs to be brought under control. I live by this and it is a great reminder for whenever I see myself or someone else not acting according to the superhero standard of best self. In the end, if the relationship is genuine and valuable, you will trust those people the same as the superhero trusts the content and the source of the communication.

There is nothing worse than the wrong information being communicated or the right information being interpreted incorrectly. Effective communication involves both parties making sure that there is understanding from the communication and that nothing can be left to interpretation. We see this a lot in our jobs and in our homes. There's a funny meme out there that has a wife asking her husband to go shopping. She asks him to go to the store to buy milk and then says, "if they have avocados, buy six!". The husband returns home with six gallons of milk and says "they had avocados". Now we can correctly assume that the wife meant that if the store had avocados, for the husband to buy six avocados. However, she never said to buy avocados so I'm going out on a limb to say that the husband took her request as some type of omen which led to him misinterpreting her request to buy six gallons of milk if the store has avocados. That makes absolutely no sense but logically the request was left open for interpretation. We go through this a lot with our children and in the fast food drive through. We can see instructions given without clarity which can lead to a process being followed incorrectly and a negative or wrong result/impact obtained. Clarity not only involves the who, what, when, where, & why of effective communication but it also involves that the receiving party understands the message clearly and asks the right questions to gain a clear understanding.

Most helmets, especially military helmets, are equipped with a communication system. A soldier is able to listen to any commands or updates that are coming through that system. Trouble awaits if the message is not clear or understandable. Ultimate disaster awaits if the wrong person gets a hold of the coms and starts speaking the incorrect message into your ear. The key of effective communication is that it drives powerful connections and gives direction. The mind is the target. The helmet protects the mind from a physical attack however the communication system acts as a sensory and mental protector. What you hear and who you hear it from is vital to your success as a superhero.

CHAPTER XI

Becoming The Superhero Of You

"Neither a wise or a brave man lies down on the tracks and waits for the train of the future to run over him."
— Dwight D Eisenhower

We have seen plenty of movies and read plenty of fictional books about an overzealous scientist trying to build the ultimate superhero. Ultimately, we see that creation turn into the evil antagonist. The reason why the created hero changes is because the wrong intentions went into its creation. The attempted hero did have values and attributes, it's just that those values and characteristics were distorted. The standard was not 100% authentic or genuine to the unwavering and absolute truth.

The superhero that you build cannot be created quickly. You also cannot take pieces that you like and try to dump them into your superhero and expect perfection. Building a true and authentic superhero takes time to develop. It's likened to forging raw gold into a high-quality piece of jewelry. There are going to be ups, downs, hard times, slow times, fun times, right times, and wrong times. Each time however, develops the character. Those times are not a waste. It has to happen in order for the superhero to build great attributes while at the same time getting rid of bad ones.

You have excellence and greatness inside you, and you were not put on earth to live a life of mediocrity. Do not wait for a superhero to show up, become one yourself. Why wait when you have the ability to fly high and leap far. Take risk and lead with some common sense. Live like there's no tomorrow with the pursuit of living forever. Pursue greatness, choose excellence, and be a superhero. As you create the superhero of You, remember to mold your attributes to an unwavering absolute standard. Who are you going to be and why? What are you going to stand for? Who are you going to save?

To get started, all you need is the belief that you can be a superhero and trust the process of molding into one. You do not even need all the faith at the start, because faith can be strengthened as you pursue and grow. You're going to make mistakes, you may disappoint yourself, you may want to give up, you're going to have setbacks, you'll even experience failures, but if you embrace failure, believe that you can become, and put forth the effort, you will be a superhero.

Let me get one thing surely straight as a reminder. Superheroes are not born, they are developed. One thing for sure, the superheroes we love and follow, their past is pretty much no mystery. They were not destined at birth to be a superhero. Almost all have experienced some tragic background which became the springboard to their superhero development. When they finally realized and weathered their storms...well then you see who they are. So, don't harp on your past. Your past doesn't hold you; you hold it. Letting your past hold you prevents you from moving forward.

Who are you? Yes, I just ask you that question and I'll ask again. Who are you? You've just read what the basics are to building your superhero. We all need you to answer this question. Who are you? And I do not mean the obvious. I want you to search for yourself. Search deep down in your soul. Go past the surface created by other people's versions of you, go past those corrupt belief systems. Go past the you that was created because of what somebody negatively said you were years ago. Go past the negative you that was created because of a tragic event. Go past the negative voices screaming at you. Don't listen to those voices. Go past the voices that called you names and picked on you. Go past the voices of those who say they love you but have set limitations on you. The ones who said, "you can't" or "you'll never be able to" or my favorite, "I don't know what gave you that idea". Yeah, don't listen to these voices.

I want you to look in the mirror and hear your true voice. That voice may be muffled at first but it's the one that tells you "you are able", "you can be anything you want", "you can achieve anything you set out to be", "you are strong, you are beautiful, you are divinely created!" Just as important, listen to the voices around you that confirm that truth and inspire you to become that voice. Listen to the voices that solidify your foundation and allow you to start your journey with confidence. Listen to those voices that allow you to put on each one of the pieces and wear them without fear of shame, guilt or doubt. Listen to the voice that confirms your absolute truth, your SUPERHERO.

Live like a hero. That's what the classics teach us. Be a main character. Otherwise what is life for? – J.M. Coetzee

Congratulations!

You're building
A SUPERHERO!

Ephesians 6:13 - 18

Therefore, put on the full armor of God, so that when the day of evil comes, you may be able to stand your ground, and after you have done everything, to stand. Stand firm then, with the belt of truth buckled around your waist, with the breastplate of righteousness in place, and with your feet fitted with the readiness that comes from the gospel of peace. In addition to all this, take up the shield of faith, with which you can extinguish all the flaming arrows of the evil one. Take the helmet of salvation and the sword of the Spirit, which is the word of God. And pray in the Spirit on all occasions with all kinds of prayers and requests.

Let's Build!

Taking what you've just read; I want you to visualize your superhero self.

    Who would that hero be?

    What would he/she look like?

    Are you mystical?

    Are you an animal?

    Which superhero can serve as your base?

What is your truth?

How To Build A Superhero

What are your positive character traits and attributes?

Draw your Superhero.
Be Creative!
Be You!

How To Build A Superhero

Jason E Oliver

Describe Your Superhero.

How To Build A Superhero

What are your Superpowers?

How To Build A Superhero

I love it!
Now go be heroic!

How To Build A Superhero

About The Author
Jason E Oliver

Jason E Oliver, a New York native, is a servant, leader, author, mentor, coach, speaker, and business owner. Jason has worked in many industries and has gained many life experiences. Some joyful, some not so much. In all, he has found that his greatest joy has always come from serving others.

Jason's unique purpose is to make you realize that no matter how big or how small, you are a Superhero and should live life as your best self. He believes that the path to your best self takes #ROADWORK. These are the tools needed for Change in order to Know Your Self, & Understand Your What and Your Why.

Jason is a certified life coach as well as Lean Six Sigma certified and utilizes techniques to help people improve and make successful shifts in their thinking, habits, and actions. Jason keeps a positive outlook and believes that all things happen for our growth and eventual success. Many have sought after him for inspiration and as he states "I am inspired by everyone who wants to find a better way".

www.ingramcontent.com/pod-product-compliance
Lightning Source LLC
Chambersburg PA
CBHW062149100526
44589CB00014B/1747